I0453787

Elevate Your Resume

Tips for Accelerating Your Career

Heather Michelle Harmon

Global Window Publishing—Chattanooga, TN
ISBN: 979-8-218-15892-7
Library of Congress Control Number: 2023904407
Elevate Your Resume: Tips for Accelerating Your Career
Author: Heather Michelle Harmon
Digital distribution | 2023
Paperback | 2023

Dedication

To my husband and daughters, let this book serve as a reminder that you can accomplish whatever you set your mind to, and the fastest way to finish anything in life is to get started.

Table of Contents

Introduction

This book was made for experienced professionals, skilled in their chosen field, looking for career advancement, who have determined their career trajectory. It will give you practical application ideas and examples that you can put into practice immediately to further your career aspirations and climb the proverbial ladder.

This book is not written for first time job applicants, entry-level employees with little to no work experience, and/or those who haven't determined their North Star goal/career trajectory, however, there are chapters they can put into practice to enhance their professional image as well as tips to begin planning their career aspirations.

Getting promoted to management or even executive leadership means shifting from an emphasis on day-to-day operations to a more long-term, strategic perspective. Leaders at this level often manage multiple teams, although they may also function as standalone experts. The requirements for advancement to the next level are stringent. You'll need to demonstrate your competence in the position before you'll be given official recognition for it, and when you do, no one should be surprised because you will have earned it. To achieve this lofty goal, one must put in extra effort on top of an already hectic schedule and have the fortitude to persevere when things don't go as planned. Assess whether this goal matches your North Star goals.

If you're promoted, what new responsibilities will you have? What would your daily schedule look like? Do you see yourself doing this job on a daily basis? When you take on more, you'll be taking on more pressure, more work, and more responsibility. It's all doable, but how does it compare to what really matters to you?

- What do you hope to accomplish from your promotion?
- Do you believe these outcomes will serve as continued motivation when things get difficult?
- And, more importantly, are you prepared to make the necessary sacrifices to realize these goals?

Have you shown a track record of making a significant strategic contribution to the success of your team, your department, or your clients? What other ways have you contributed to projects beyond the financial impact on the company's bottom line? In what ways have you promoted responsible business practices as a company? Many applicants consider just the effects on the customers they serve and therefore fail to take into account the views of their colleagues and customers upstream and downstream from them, who can often tout your contributions.

Are you an example for others to follow in terms of your strategic, reputational, and people-leading conduct and methods of operation? Do you have executive sponsors (customers, stakeholders, front- and back-end leaders that rely on you) who can elaborate on the positive effects you've had in their respective domains? In today's world, it's not enough to just know people; you also need to be known by those who have significant power.

Do a Google search for resume writing or interview tips and you'll find tons of basic information but more advanced professionals with existing experience need to up their game to be considered for higher paying, more advanced roles. This book helps you answer the aforementioned questions and goes beyond common sense advice to give you more tools that set you apart from your competition as well as effective ways to enhance your professional reputation and resume.

Chapter One
North Star Goals

North Star goals are the top of the pyramid, a Mount Everest expedition of sorts. Mariners defer to the sky's North Star to guide them if/when they get off track because of its due north consistency aligning with the North Pole axis and remains stationary while other stars rotate, meaning it can always be counted on. Goals work the same way, you should have an end-result goal called the North Star goal and everything else you do should be pointing you in that intentional direction.

Creating professional goals is an important step in advancing your career and achieving long-term success. Professional goals help you to define your aspirations, clarify your direction, and measure your progress. All goals should be inching you closer to your North Star goals. Here's how and why to create professional goals (note that personal goals have the same attributes):

1. **Set a clear direction:** Setting professional goals gives you a clear direction for where you want to go in your career. By identifying your goals, you can create a plan of action to achieve them, and stay focused on the path that will lead you to success.

2. **Measure your progress:** Goals help you to measure your progress and determine whether you are on track to achieving your objectives. This helps you to stay motivated and focused, and also allows you to adjust your plan if necessary.

3. **Develop skills:** Setting professional goals can help you to develop new skills and enhance your existing ones. By identifying the skills you need to achieve your goals, you can create a plan to acquire them through training, education, or hands-on experience.

4. **Enhance your performance:** Goals help you to enhance your performance by giving you a clear target to aim for. By working towards your goals, you can improve your productivity, efficiency, and quality of work.

5. **Achieve long-term success:** Professional goals help you to achieve long-term success by providing a roadmap for your career. By

setting goals that align with your values and aspirations, you can create a fulfilling and rewarding career that brings you personal and professional satisfaction.

To create goals, personal and professional, start by identifying your values, interests, and aspirations. Then, determine what you want to achieve personally or in your career, and set specific, measurable, achievable, relevant, and time-bound (SMART) goals that align with your vision. Finally, create a plan of action that outlines the steps you need to take to achieve your goals, and track your progress along the way.

Deliberately planning for your future self now, as in learning skills, is an excellent plan so your future self will be qualified for your North Star goal. **We do this so we can be ready for opportunities when they come up in the future.** For instance, if your North Star goal is to be a CFO, you'd be preparing by studying accounting practices and getting experience in accounting roles to someday be eligible for the CFO position.

Asking yourself, "Who do I want to be?" is the first step toward creating a workable plan for your future. "Where do I want to go?" helps you delve even deeper. Likely, the responses to these questions will point toward future development. You might not achieve everything on your list but you're guaranteed not to change if you don't deliberately try. Planning for your future self is an action plan for achieving goals.

For instance, if you want to become a writer, you must, of course, spend a lot of time writing. It is not enough to be a good salesperson if you want to advance into a management position in sales. Building your knowledge and experience is essential if you want to start a business, introduce a new product, or take charge of a team. You're not going to be able to get a promotion and make more money by continuing to do the exact same thing you're doing now.

Here's the catch: you need to invest in the future even if other, more pressing tasks are piling up right now, and there doesn't seem to be any clear payoff for your time spent. To get things done, you have to deliberately spend time on activities that have the potential to benefit your future self, as opposed to the immediate benefit now. Think of it like tending to a garden, you plant seeds for the future knowing it won't sprout immediately.

We all need a reason to push us forward, whether it is personal or professional development. Knowing your "why" can act as an anchor that propels you through life. But what exactly does knowing your why mean? It means understanding our driving force and the motivations behind our goals in both our careers and lives outside of work. Having an inner compass guides us towards decisions that are true to ourselves, strengthens relationships with others, and provides a source of resilience when things get hard.

Start with a vision board, I prefer written words over pictures alone, but giving yourself something to see on a regular basis is the point. Use the template included or another means of articulating your goals. This helps hold yourself responsible and should remind you to say no to things that distract you from your chosen goals. I categorize my goals because I distinguish personal from professional goals as both matter to me, then I attach visual representations of my goals underneath my written goals to help remind and motivate me. For instance, I wanted a professional job where I felt respected so I attached pictures of business attire for women cut out of magazines. A personal goal was to travel more with my family so I attached pictures of cruise ships.

What are your goals? Write them down and actively work towards them. Break them into smaller pieces if the goal is lofty, you'll feel more accomplished. What is your Why? Do you want good work/life balance because of your family? Do you want a powerful, high paying position with lots of responsibilities? Know your Why – your motivation, what drives you.

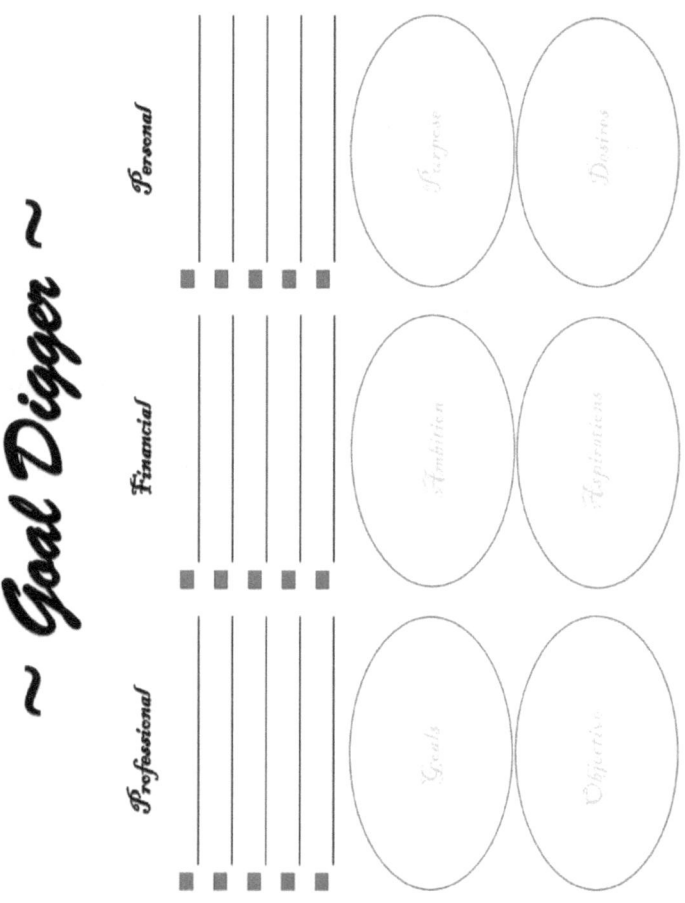

Chapter Two

Resume Magic

Resumes (and profiles such as LinkedIn) are supposed to be a summary of what you've done professionally, but tailored to the specific role/industry you're in. It's considered a living document, meaning it will constantly change and evolve. While there's no single one way to make a perfect resume, there are basic best practices such as not including a picture, listing accomplishments instead of duties, and utilizing key words from the job description.

Are you feeling a bit stuck when it comes to crafting an impressive resume that stands out from the competition? If so, you're not alone! One of the greatest challenges job seekers face is summarizing all their accomplishments onto one or two pages. With only limited space and no room for error, how can you make sure your background, skillset, and experience truly shine through in just a few sentences? The answer lies in storytelling – building compelling stories around your resume accomplishments.

Storytelling allows recruiters to draw key points directly from those tales and really understand who the person behind them is. It also puts any dry facts into perspective by giving readers more of an understanding on what sort of situation they occurred under and why this matters overall. As such, instead of simply listing your achievements as bullet points or writing tired phrases like "achieved success in roles with increasing responsibility", or "responsible for...", be creative - pick between 1-3 specific bullet-point successes that best demonstrate each particular role; then expand those into detailed stories which take these items further (e.g., timeframe involved / difficulties encountered / budgets obtained). By doing so, recruiters will gain valuable insight into your capabilities almost instantly whilst showing off how well you collaborate & communicate info quickly too!

Have you ever noticed how job descriptions are in present tense verbiage? It makes sense, they're looking for someone with current, existing skills, right? But why would you be looking for the same exact job you already have? If you're like most people, you're looking to advance your career, not stagnate by jumping from one job to the exact same job somewhere else. Your current role should be in the present tense and your previous jobs should be in the past tense; but what if your experience was in a prior role? With Application Tracking Software

(ATS), basically electronic resume bots tasked with weeding out people who aren't qualified, you have to figure out a way to get your resume past those gatekeepers so you can explain how your experience is relevant. How do you do that if you don't have the exact experience currently or your skills are more transferable? Great question!

I've been writing resumes for almost 20 years, fine tuning my method and experimenting with what works and what doesn't work. Over the years I've evolved my template (as one should always be doing) and now have a template that has a fairly high success rate of getting past the gatekeepers and getting noticed by the recruiters enough to get an interview. While the applicants themselves had to ace the interview, my resumes have helped many people get the interview for very high paying jobs (some paying more than $100,000 annually). That's the whole point of a resume; a written document that convinces a recruiter or hiring manager to select you for an interview, getting you one step closer to getting the job. The following categories are the sections my resume template includes, and each section has a specific purpose in tailoring the resume to the requirements of the job you are seeking, I use it in this order but if you wanted to downplay an area, such as Education, you may choose to move that section to the bottom. On average, hiring managers only look at a resume for 6 seconds and most of that time is spent skimming the top half - so your most impactful information should be close to the top.

- Pertinent Contact Information
- Synonymous job titles
- Objective
- Highlights of Expertise
- Education
- Direct Experience
- Professional Experience

Pertinent Contact Information should go without saying, but I'll say it anyway just in case. Your name should be bold enough to see first and include the city/state you reside in, your phone number, and relevant professional sites like LinkedIn (perhaps more if you're in a creative role or have a digital portfolio that further highlights your experience or skills). Of course, keep it simple; simple font, simple formatting, simple layout.

| Mickey Mouse, MBA | Orlando, Florida ▪ 555-666-7777 |
| | MickeyMouseMBA@hotmail.com ▪ www.linkedin.com/in/mickey-mouse-mba |

Synonymous Job Titles are interesting because we've found a way to trick the system. Remember how I mentioned ATS robots are looking for present tense key words, like titles, in your resume? Again, unless you're looking to hop from one position to the same exact position somewhere else, you wouldn't necessarily have this title in your job history. The work around is to have this small, but powerful, section that gives us those present tense titles to put on our resume that we may not otherwise have, these are aspirational titles so they should be similar to one another. The ATS bots see the aspiring job titles as a title match. One crisis averted!

SENIOR ANALYST | STRATEGY ANALYST | REPORTING CONSULTANT | DIRECTOR OF CORPORATE STRATEGY

The **Objective** section gets mixed reviews, some believe it should be on the resume and others think it is outdated and self-serving. Personally, I believe it can be used to succinctly include information that may not otherwise be included, such as X years in X industry (which is extremely valuable if there is a minimum experience clause in the job description. This could be a great way to include a relevant accolade and/or impressive accomplishment, which can be stated in story form to entice the recruiter (as long as it is relevant to the position and highlights a solution to a perceived pain point and/or skill).

Results-driven, growth-oriented professional with 10+ years' experience in business management and non-profit civic organizations. Expert at planning and setting long-term strategic plans, as well as optimizing organizational efficiency, reducing cost, and surpassing business objectives. Recently analyzed an organizational survey or the future direction of the organization; presented results and recommendations in a strategic analysis report for stakeholders; results of the analysis were used to inform 5-year strategic plan.

Next is the **Highlights of Expertise** section where we again get to fill in our resume with key words, sprinkling them in with finesse. Once again, the ATS software is most likely looking for present tense verbiage that is hard to say in a prior role since we'd be using past tense to describe what we did BACK THEN. Make sure to include your superpower as well as applicable skills that are relevant to the new position. Richard Branson (Founder and CEO of Virgin) said, "If somebody offers you an amazing opportunity but you are not sure you can do it, say yes – then learn how to do it later!" If there are skills required that you aren't experienced with, I suggest taking a power course on YouTube, Coursera, Lynda.com, etc. so you can gain exposure to that skill and show interest in learning more about it, not to mention put it on your resume! Here's a hint, if it's a required skill it 100% has to be on your resume, but don't pretend to be an expert if you're not. It is perfectly acceptable to put "Exposed to" or "Experience with [insert required skill here]". This is simply another place to match keywords that hiring managers, or more likely ATS bots, are looking for. If you don't have enough of them, your resume is automatically getting tossed in the *not qualified enough* section and won't be looked at again. DO NOT LIE. If you don't have experience, go get some! There's no excuse not to with all of the free resources on the internet. If you want something bad enough, you'll do whatever it takes, like learn a new skill quickly to be qualified.

Highlights of Expertise		
• Strategic Forecasting and Planning	• Experience with Power BI & Tableau	• Microsoft Access
• Project Management skills	• Strategy and Program Evaluation	• Benchmark Productivity
• Advanced Microsoft Excel skills	• Advanced Excel & Data Analytics	• Dashboard Building

Education should be self-explanatory, if there is a minimum education requirement, you'll want to point that out, more than likely they'll be searching for it as a pre-requisite to anything else on your resume. If you don't have a higher education or relevant professional credential you may want to move this section to the very bottom of your resume to downplay it, especially if it's of little importance for the specific role. This is another section where you DO NOT LIE, if you're in the process of obtaining a degree or credential, include the word Pending with an anticipated completion date (month and year), this is a trick that will check off the requirement and may allow you to get to the interview where you can plead your case and show interest/ability directly to the hiring director who may overlook the lack of a 100% completed requirement. You'll never know what the hiring manager may be willing to budge on unless you can get far enough in the interview process to find out.

Education		
Master of Business Administration	12/2017	University of Central Florida, Orlando, FL
Bachelor of Public Administration	5/2015	University of Central Florida, Orlando, FL
Associate of Accounting & Business Administration	6/2012	University of Central Florida, Orlando, FL

My favorite section of the resume is the **Direct Experience** section because this is where we get to brag about our most impressive accomplishments, relevant to the position of course. First, I analyze the role values in terms of overarching skills, then I figure out how my past experience aligns with those values. I like to choose 3 or 4 main categories that I can see are of importance for the specific role (such as Leadership, Communication, Data Analysis, Management, Project Management etc.) and use the categorized bullet points to prove I have that specific experience (that's how I tell the story, the categories/stories should be somewhat related and flow seamlessly). This is the SHOW and TELL part of the resume, you tell them you have the skills, then you show/prove it with specific examples. I want my resume to say, "BAM! I'm the perfect candidate for this role and here's why." Do you have an Accomplishments/Brag folder that helps recollect a project you were on, a problem you solved, or processes you improved? If not, you should. Remember to summarize them using the STAR method (Situation, Task, Action, Result). Use metrics if you can, a good resume should have at least 5 metrics (such as % increase/decrease, $ increase/decrease, X improvement, etc.). What I love about this section is we don't have to identify how recent this experience was, we're just highlighting the most relevant experience that is directly related to the role, so it doesn't matter if it was for an older role 10+ years ago, a volunteer position, internship, or task force we were on. We did the work, we get to take credit for it, and now we get to humble brag about it (not taking sole credit if it was a group effort might I add).

Direct Experience

Data Analysis:
- Advanced Knowledge of MS Excel 2010, 2013, & 2016 Formulas and Functions, such as Pivot Tables, What-If Analysis, VLOOKUP function, Power Pivot, etc.
- Strong presentation skills with Microsoft Office 2007, 2010, 3013, & 2016 software, including Microsoft Word, Excel, PowerPoint, Publisher, Access, and Outlook
- Data Visualization Tools including Tableau, Power Pivot, Power Query, SQL based queries, Power BI
- Experience with POS and ERP Software, such as Eclipse, SAP, Microsoft Dynamics GP & SL, SBA, Salesforce, and QuickBooks

Operations Management:
- Analyzed demographic & economic market data to identify trends and forecast effective strategies
- Conducted organizational study, including data collection, analysis, and feedback; presented results and recommendations in a strategic analysis report for future strategic planning purposes
- Identified and built relationships with potential donors, contacted corporate representatives and community leaders to increase awareness of organizational causes, activities, and needs
- Developed and implemented strategies to encourage new or increased contributions, monitored progress, and secured commitments of participation and/or donations

Project Management:
- Coordinated events and logistics with advanced preparation as well as adeptly set and tracked project costs and productivity benchmarks
- Collected and analyzed data using calculations, graphical projection models, and other methods as necessary to understand current operations and determine areas for improvement
- Developed and updated system procedures as needed to address changing operational requirements and documented changes; tested procedures to keep system information accurate and productive

---

Begin with creating bullet points of accomplishments - then categorize them (they can have multiple categories if applicable), this step will help later on when highlighting your most pertinent experience that shows the recruiter you'd be perfect for the job. When being interviewed, you can easily come up with an example of the question being asked because you're preparing for it now.

Lastly, we include what recruiters are expecting to see, a reverse chronological list of our **Professional Experience**, starting with our most recent role. We can summarize what the company or organization does as a whole (Hint - this is an excellent place to include some metrics if your resume is lacking some elsewhere). You can incorporate your departments' metrics into your personal pitch when referring to your current position, be sure to include what your personal contribution is to those metrics as well. I like to use this in the brief description about the company on my resume, under which I include my personal contributions in bullet point form. This tactic has the added benefit of incorporating quantifiable results. Make sure to include your position title (using synonymous titles if necessary and applicable unless going for a promotion at your current place of employment, however, you can list more than 1 job title for a single job if the work you did was comparable to another title as well) as well as month and year (starting date to Current is acceptable if you're currently in that position as there would be no end date).

Your personal contribution should highlight accomplishments above and beyond your job duties. This could include some of the department metrics if you personally contributed to them, otherwise point out efficiencies you made and how that contribution made a difference in your position. Keep in mind you're not recreating a job post so don't list job duties, if you are then you need to spend more time thinking about your specific contribution to the role. Do make sure to incorporate action words in your resume, as opposed to using passive verbs.

It's not enough to have a great resume though, you also have to cultivate professional social networks and build credibility over time too.

Chapter Three
Visibility in the Workplace

Increase your visibility by shining a light on your abilities.

It can be difficult to find ways to stand out at work, it's all too easy to slip into the background. A number of factors can lead to feeling invisible at work: whether you are remote or co-located, take a junior or senior role, or have a proactive or reactive personality.

You might sometimes feel invisible in your job, and even when you are eager to step forward and share your ideas, you might worry about appearing arrogant or annoying to your coworkers. Don't be afraid to put yourself forward, even when working remotely or in a team of equals. **Utilize these strategies to gain visibility in the workplace without feeling like others have to lose in order for you to win.**

Why should you be more visible?

To rise to the top in one's field, visibility is crucial. People are more inclined to consider you for promotions or interesting assignments if they know who you are and what you're capable of. And those who keep their head down often miss out, despite their hard work.

If you want to be considered for chances when they emerge, you need to take the initiative to raise your profile as much as possible, rather than waiting for others (like your employer) to do it for you. This is especially important if you work remotely and don't often see others in your organization.

How to Improve Your Visibility in the Workplace

Use these strategies to improve your visibility (**AND CONFIDENCE**) within your organization:

STRATEGY + ACTION = RESULTS

DELIBERATELY STRENGTHEN RELATIONSHIPS

Think like a boss, look at the department and/or company big picture, align your goals/KPI's to the bigger picture and draw a connection between your work. Intentionally work on strengthening or developing relationships with your boss, coworkers, customers, and others in your network.

- Take copious notes about your connections (about their personal life, things they wish to share with you, communication preferences, etc.).
- Help others when you can without expecting anything in return.
- Ask for stretch assignments from your boss.

When you take a personal interest in your connections you automatically strengthen bonds. Do this intentionally and see your relationships grow. Do enough for others and when you're in need of their help, they'll likely jump to your aid.

WORK SMARTER, NOT HARDER

Be efficient with your time and gain some of it back. Would time blocking (on your calendar) help? Can processes be automated to free up additional time?

- Utilize tools that make your job faster/more efficient.
- Learn new skills to improve and/or streamline some aspects of your work (such as Outlook).
- Make meetings more productive (create an agenda and disburse it with each meeting invite to keep discussions on task).

Being efficient is more than just a skill, it will help you free up time to take on additional tasks or learn new skills. We all have 1,440 minutes available in a day, what is the difference between those who are successful and those who struggle? It probably has a lot to do with how they utilize their time.

DEMONSTRATE YOUR EXPERTISE

You can raise your profile by sharing what you know. You could write a blog or contribute to a newsletter. You could also offer to conduct training sessions or share your expertise at company events, which immediately elevates your visibility.

- Identify your professional superpower (you probably have more than one).
- Seek out opportunities to utilize your skills – don't wait to be assigned, ASK for it when you hear about something you're interested in.

After developing a reputation of having specific skills, others may ask for your help directly. Over time, you may be positioned as the go-to expert for various skills, as well as lead to projects that expand your experience and visibility.

ACTIVELY PARTICIPATE IN MEETINGS

Meetings are excellent opportunities to demonstrate your knowledge and boost your visibility within your team or department. Preparation is the key to overcoming fear of public speaking and/or feeling rejected.

- Speak up, actively be engaged in the conversation.
- Come **PREPARED** with ideas.
- Only participate if you have something to offer and it's of value to your work – otherwise send someone else or opt out.

Read the agenda before a meeting and prepare your questions and/or points. This will give you the confidence you need to speak up in meetings. Actively engaging in meetings will help boost your visibility as being knowledgeable as well as collaborative.

PARTICIPATE IN LEARNING OPPORTUNITIES

Training events for the company, such as "lunch and learn" sessions offer great opportunities for you to increase your knowledge in addition to learning more about your colleagues.

- Get involved in networks such as Toast Masters or industry organizations.
- Secondary degrees, what interests you? What will help you grow in your career?

- Courses (LinkedIn, Lynda.com, Udemy, edX, Coursera, etc.)
- ALWAYS BE LEARNING!

You're more likely to find opportunities arise when you're out looking for them, as opposed to passively waiting for them to find you.

VOLUNTEER

Are there opportunities for you to network with other team members, or try your hand at outside projects that have an impact on your team's goals or on your organization as a whole?

You can be volunTOLD or you can volunteer for assignments above and beyond your job description. These new tasks can help you achieve visibility as well as expand your skill sets.

- Volunteer to represent your team or department, maybe make a presentation for a quarterly meeting.
- Volunteer for speaking engagements (even if it's out of your comfort zone).
- Volunteer for stretch assignments.
- Volunteer your services to others – this is the fastest way to gain visibility.

By sharing your expertise, your profile will grow even further. You might write a regular blog or contribute to a newsletter, offer to train people, or speak at conferences, instantly increasing your value as well as your visibility.

ASK FOR VISIBLE PROJECTS

Are there any assignments you can take on that have a significant impact on the bottom line of your organization? Do you work with people from other teams or departments? The bigger the impact, the bigger the visibility.

- Ask for big impact assignments/projects that matter to your organization.
- Volunteer for cross-departmental projects to gain visibility.

This will demonstrate your leadership ability and help you build even more new relationships that help expand your visibility as well as new skill sets.

GROW YOUR NETWORK

If you take the time to build and nurture relationships, you'll create a strong network of allies. Your network is bigger than you think it is; any school (even high school or college), association (like scouts), church, or team is part of your network. Keep in contact, interact, and reach out to them. Here's a tip - **BE A RESOURCE FOR THEM TOO**.

- Consider your networking objectives and how to best reach the people you want to establish relationships with so that you can grow your network further.
- Perhaps get engaged in a leadership role with outside organizations - you get to add them to your resume! This is another place volunteering comes in handy.

This network can advocate for you to be recommended for jobs, high visibility projects, stretch assignments, promotions, etc.

How big is your network? My network consists of people I went to middle school, high school, and college with, organizations I ever worked for, and people and organizations I follow on LinkedIn. I don't need to know them personally, but the common interest is enough to call them a network. Just the other day I came across an acquaintance from middle school who posted on LinkedIn they were looking for a new job. I knew this person by name but never hung out with them in school, I assume we went to high school together too but again, we weren't friends and our paths never crossed. However, I represent the company I work for, so I told her to seek opportunities at my company and she put in an application, I even offered to look over her resume to give pointers on how to position herself in the best light possible. This has happened several times. That's how networks should work, I want to be a resource for others and people I know, or know of, are going to have a better opportunity than a complete and total stranger with no connection to me whatsoever (for instance a random person on LinkedIn I've never met also looking for a job). **So I ask again, how big is your network? It's probably bigger than you think it is.**

LAST BIT OF ADVICE

Mentors: Mentors can offer invaluable advice on getting noticed, and they can serve as sponsors for you, inside the organization as well as with outside connections. Mentors help you strategize goals and benchmark results as well as offer an outside perspective to professional challenges you may be facing.

Consistency: Your reputation, good or bad, will be as a result of the consistency you provide. Are you reliable? Are you consistently delivering high quality results on time?

It takes more than hard effort to move forward in today's highly competitive world; those who raise their profile at work are more likely to be considered for promotions.

The methods contained in this chapter can help you become more visible immediately. By doing so, you'll be able to raise your profile without coming across as conceited or inconsiderate.

Action Item:

MY GOAL IS TO....	YOUR ACTION WOULD BE
Become a better public speaker	⇒ Sign up for a public speaking course
Strengthen relationships	⇒ Go to lunch with my mom
Negotiate for a higher salary	⇒ Create a plan of action to create value
Have a better work/life balance	⇒ Block off time in my work calendar

MY GOAL IS TO....	YOUR ACTION
	⇒
	⇒
	⇒
	⇒

- What visibility actions do you want to take in the next 3 months?
- How will you do it? Break down the steps.
- By when? Set milestones, with specific dates.
- What additional support/resources do you need?

Don't forget to define your Goals & Actions!

Chapter Four
Swot Analysis

Do you remember the very beginning of the animated movie, Hercules (where Hercules shows so much strength but is overzealous about utilizing his strength that he knocks down a whole town and is made fun of)? Like Hercules, we have to learn to figure out what our strengths are, then use them in a productive way. At the beginning, no one liked Hercules because he was so strong, we can presume when he was younger he may have showed off his strength and expected to be liked for it (by imagining events leading up to the kids being afraid of his overbearing strength).

So rather than show off what our strengths are, or we're really good at, we need to figure out how to utilize our strengths in strategic ways. Of course, we can have many strengths, but we want to position ourselves as the go-to expert for something, if we can.

Exercise:

Similar to a SWOT Analysis, I made this to analyze our Strengths, Weaknesses, and Tools we use now vs. Tools we don't use now but could.

- Not only do we want to identify our strengths, but we also want to describe how we use them, who they benefit and how, and how we might be able to expand them to be even more impactful.

- Then we want to list our weaknesses, but it's not enough to just list them, we also want to identify how these are holding us back, how we can practice turning them into strengths, and what is the result of these weaknesses holding us back.

- Next we look at the tools we utilize, what we like about them, dislike, and how can we make what we already use more efficient.

- Last, but not least, we want to research tools we don't currently use but could. How could we utilize them, what would they improve, and what is stopping us from utilizing these tools?

Most of us were brought up to believe that our accomplishments were the best barometer of our worth. To that extent, one may say that performance and a strength are synonymous, but our gut tells us that's not the case. Like most individuals, you probably have certain things you're good at, yet you dread doing. You're capable of doing it but it's a draining experience, and you wish you'd never have to do it again. Clearly, actions like this are not strengths. In other words, they are flaws. A strength is best understood as "something you do that makes you stronger." In fact, a weakness is defined as "anything you do that weakens you," even if you happen to be brilliant at it. You have to decide for yourself how much energy you should be expending and if it's worth it to you or not. Somethings come more naturally to us, therefore they require less energy and we either gravitate towards them or naturally shy away from them.

Now when you fill in this spreadsheet, you can identify your strengths and weaknesses in terms of energy and what energizes you versus what drains you. What are you naturally good at or what skills did you pick up easily? Just because you're good at something doesn't mean you like doing it. Women may be "good" at getting coffee and setting up meetings because their organization skills may be perceived to be better than men but that doesn't mean it provides high value and those skills won't elevate you for a promotion.

Strengths	Weaknesses
1	1
2	2
3	3
4	4
5	5
How do you use them?	Why are these holding you back?
Who do these skills benefit and how?	How can you practice turning these into strengths?
How can you expand these strengths to be even more impactful?	What is the result of these weaknesses holding you back?

Tools You Utilize	New Tools You Could Try
1	1
2	2
3	3
4	4
5	5
What do you like about these tools?	How would you utilize them?
What do you dislike about these tools?	What would they improve?
What can you do to make these tools more efficient?	What is holding you back from trying these?

The point to this exercise is to write down what we think our limitations are - this helps give ourselves accountability when we write things down. Look at this list often, contemplate how or why, amend it when needed. This is a SPECIFIC list to work from now, we've articulated areas of improvement. I'd say articulating it is half the battle.

Many years ago I was an accountant for a large non-profit organization. I had finished my associate's degree and was actively working on my bachelor's while simultaneously working (and raising kids!), then continued to finish my master's while in the same position. In school, of course you utilize the latest software for classes and are learning current skills -- so I had learned Excel tricks as part of my schooling and as a result became fairly proficient. My coworkers, however, were a little older than I was, one by a few years and had been out of college for around 10 years, the other one was my parents age and had been out of college for a good 15 or 20 years so their technology skills were not as recent as mine. Perhaps I was overzealous in sharing my skills but I was surprised accountants were doing a lot of unnecessary manual work, as opposed to using pivot tables to combine information. I showed them how to use pivot tables and other Excel tricks here and there when I thought it could help - I didn't want to overwhelm them by showing them every single tool they could use but they were more comfortable with their existing manual processes.

As a result of the skills I had acquired, and once I learned the existing system, I was able to start taking on more tasks and making them more efficient so I could take on more responsibilities. This had the end result of unburdening the senior accountant so she could do more analyzing and forecasting, while positioning me as a go-to expert (lose term) for that specific tool. I leveraged my Excel skills and continued to learn new skills that could be even more beneficial in that role. While my skills were never herald as was Hercules', my end goal wasn't to become a real life hero, however, my goal was to have the skills I acquired make processes more efficient. By the time I left, I told my boss they would need at least 2 people to fill my position since I had taken on so many new tasks. She dismissed my opinion, and a year later was still dealing with the repercussions. In truth we had needed another person in that department years before I left but because of efficient measures, I was eventually able to take on so many additional tasks myself. **This brings me to another point -- bosses don't always know the specific work we're working on so we have to let them know.** We have to find ways to tell them (performance reviews, include them on emails about you taking on new tasks, summarizing the end result, etc.), that's why it is extremely important to have a running document listing additional tasks, small and large projects, efficiency measures, new tools, etc.

We need to work strategically - that means:
- Doing something new
- Building on what you already do
- Reacting opportunistically to emerging possibilities

Pay attention to the large organization conversations, what matters to them? How does your work align to the bigger picture? How can you and your skills directly contribute to the bigger picture? Think of a rainbow, there are many tiers, see the picture at each tier and make sure it aligns. What is needed from you to get you from one tier to the next tier? Start tackling those items on the Weaknesses list, what is it going to take to make those less of a weakness for you (learning new skills, delegating, etc.)?

Make a list, or better yet a folder, to keep track of your accomplishments. I have a folder in Outlook called Accomplishments, I copy and paste emails that I've sent or received that point to a project I worked on, a summarization or document I've created, etc. This is my portfolio - if I wanted to look for another job, I'd have all these references to remind me of work projects, communication, contributions I've made, and so forth. My favorite advice: **act like you're about to take a new job/promotion and you have to train someone new to take over your job.** What could you do now to help train someone quickly? For me, it was creating a step-by-step list of recurring tasks, then hyperlinking that task to an email template, form, directions, or whatever would help make that task more efficient. I do this often because I am always open for opportunities (you should be too) and I want to be prepared if, and when, one should come available. If I'm not prepared ahead of time. I may miss out on an opportunity.

Once we have a nice list of projects we've worked on or accomplishments, we can figure out how to word them impressively on our resume and LinkedIn/professional profile. **If you're ready to work on your resume, start with this task. You've already done the work, now you just need to showcase it in a portfolio, this will help you in interviews too.**

Action Items:
1. Strengths, Weaknesses, and Tools Analysis
2. List of accomplishments/project work/contribution portfolio

Chapter Five
Stop Putting Out Fires

A re you constantly putting out fires in your position (i.e., fixing mistakes, dealing with time sensitive emergencies, getting pulled into discussions on how to fix problems, spending a lot of time searching and/or organizing your email)? Guess what? You're not able to innovate or make efficiencies when you're constantly putting out fires. At that point, you're barely keeping up.

Ever feel like (or been told) you're struggling with your current duties so how/why do you feel you'd be able to take on higher responsibilities? The truth is you have to be comfortable enough with your current duties before you'd be considered for a promotion. That means:

- Consistency in your work
- Not making mistakes
- Not forgetting steps
- Not seeming overwhelmed
- Don't wait until the last minute to start an assignment/project

- Finishing what you start

So how do we stop putting out fires?

1. **First, we concentrate on completing our existing duties and projects thoroughly, accurately, and on time.** There is a parable by Benjamin Hardy that succinctly illustrates this example:

   ○ **One Behavior Separates The Successful From The Average**
   A certain farmer had become old and ready to pass his farm down to one of his two sons. When he brought his sons together to speak about it, he told them: The farm will go to the younger son."
   The older son was furious! "What are you talking about?!" he fumed.
   The father sat patiently, thinking.
   "Okay," the father said, "I need you to do something for me. We need more stocks. Will you go to Cibi's farm and see if he has any cows for sale?"
   The older son shortly returned and reported, 'Father, Cibi has 6 cows for sale."
   The father graciously thanked the older son for his work. He then turned to the younger son and said, "I need you to do something for

me. We need more stocks. Will you go to Cibi's farm and see if he has any cows for sale?"

The younger son did as he was asked. A short while later, he returned and reported, "Father, Cibi has 6 cows for sale. Each cow will cost 2,000 rupees. If we are thinking about buying more than 6 cows, Cibi said he would be willing to reduce the price 100 rupees. Cibi also said they are getting special jersey cows next week if we aren't in a hurry, it may be good to wait. However, if we need the cows urgently, Cibi said he could deliver the cows tomorrow."

The father graciously thanked the younger son for his work. He then turned to the older son and said, "That's why your younger brother is getting the farm."

One Behavior Separates The Successful From The Average | by Benjamin Hardy, PhD | Mission.org | Medium

This is the thoroughness part, are you doing only what is asked of you or are you taking the initiative to go above and beyond? *(What characteristics did you notice of the younger son that the older son didn't have?)*

Personally, putting out fires could mean activities that drain our energy, such as fighting with toddlers to take a nap at a specific time.

A method I learned to use when my children were younger was to call nap time "quiet time" instead. Rather than using the trigger words "nap-time", they heard me say they didn't need to take a nap, they could instead play quietly (not with stimulating electronics or tv) and more often than not, they would fall asleep anyway. I approached the problem in a way that didn't drain my energy. Do you feel frantic about getting chores done, like dishes, laundry, or cooking? Perhaps you could batch tasks together, like put dinner in the crockpot and wash dishes on a morning break. Don't feel like everything has to get done immediately and all at once but do a couple of small tasks around the same time and maybe not all chores need to get done every day. For instance, I don't have the time, energy, or capacity to mow my lawn every other week, so I outsource it. It unburdens me to know that a chore is getting done and I can work simultaneously. Some tasks are unavoidable, but it will help to alleviate the workload. When I walk into the kitchen, I may unload the dishwasher/dry rack then go back to work, the next time I go in I may wash just the plates in the sink.

The point is to break your chores into bite sized pieces and do a little at a time, much like we do with our work tasks. Compartmentalize if/when you need to hyper focus on your task at hand, sometimes trying to multi-task too many things actually slow us down.

2. **Secondly, we look for ways to make those existing responsibilities more efficient so we can handle them with ease. There are a few basic tools that most, if not all of us, utilize on a regular basis - Outlook, Word, and maybe Excel. It behooves us to have at least a basic understanding of these tools and then as we become more comfortable with them, we can start learning advanced features in these applications that make an impact over time. This is one example of the preparation we need which will help us be ready for opportunities when they come up in the future. Action items include:**

   ○ Create a step-by-step map of each task you have (very helpful if they are somewhat repetitive), I like to make this a checklist if I can.

- Where is the bottleneck in your processes?
- What step takes you the longest? Are there steps you dread? Can any pieces be automated?
- **It helps to think about how you would train someone new to do your job - how can you help get them up to speed in the quickest time possible?**

3. **Third, we determine new skills/tools we need to learn to be qualified for the promotion or new job) we're seeking. Does your North Star position require specific experience that you don't have yet? Is there a new software you need to learn and practice on?**

- Do you recall earlier when I talked about the preparation we need to do that will help us be ready for opportunities when they come up in the future? If we have the future in mind, we can work backwards. We can literally CREATE the experience we don't yet have so we can SHOW experience when we otherwise wouldn't have any yet. Teach yourself something, go online and watch videos of a skill you'd like to implement, then practice utilizing it, experiment with it, even volunteer to take on stretch assignments where you can utilize it in a practical application. *(What are other resources can you think of to learn new skills?)*

Right now, I'd guess you're in the second step. You're probably not 1st-day-on-the-job-brand-new, so you should have an idea of what your duties and responsibilities are. Write them down; during the course of an average month, what tasks are you assigned with completing? Break them down into step-by-step to do items and contemplate how to make them easier/faster/more efficient. Since we all have different job functions, that is an individual process.

However, there are some tools that are a little more universal and extra training could make a significant impact. Take Outlook for instance. Did you know we can automatically hide deleted meetings from our calendar without seeing the cancellation notice first? Did you know you can train Outlook to reroute emails for you? Are you aware we can batch emails together in a conversation? How about see a list of your to-do's next to your emails? Learning and using advanced tools can help unburden some manual tasks so you have more time to spend focusing on the third step - learning something new that will help advance your career. **And here's a secret - you don't always have to be learning something entirely new, gaining advanced knowledge in a tool you already** utilize can help set you apart and position you as the go-to person (elevating your status). Let me walk you thru a few examples of Outlook efficiency tips, let's see if any of these can help you. This is what I call working smarter instead of harder. Slowly and steadily, we should adopt tools that make our jobs easier.

~ Productivity tips - Outlook (2013) ~

❖ **Automatically hide cancelled meetings from calendar** – You can automatically hide canceled meetings from your view, so your calendar is always up to date, even if you haven't seen the cancellation email yet.

> **Calendar - View tab – View Settings – click Filter - go to the Advanced tab - click Field - select All Appointment fields - choose Subject - define criteria as Subject doesn't contain Canceled - click Add to List button - click OK until the panes are finished**

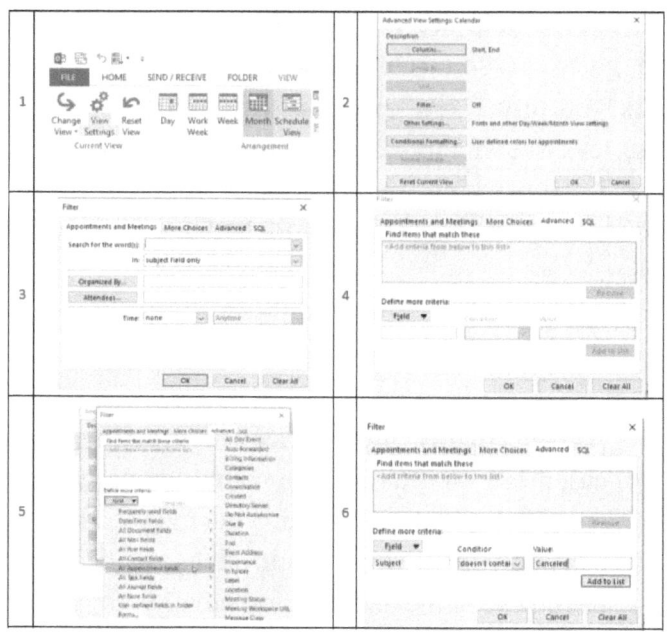

PROS	CONS
• Automatically removes cancelled meetings from your calendar	• May hide a meeting that was cancelled and rescheduled if rescheduled from a meeting that contains canceled in the subject line

❖ **Create new folders** – categorize emails by category, such as project, initiative, installation, topic, etc.), keeping your emails organized and sorted in an orderly fashion.

➢ **Right click on Inbox title on the left – select New Folder** (automatically sorted alphabetically) **– name it accordingly**

PROS	CONS
• Create and name folders based on topic (think specific project, initiative, installation, etc.) • Search has the ability to search for messages in all folders	• Folder names may be too generic, or you forget which content goes in which folder • If there's no consistency in folders, they may not be very helpful

❖ **Create rules to automatically sort messages by category -** using rules, you can automatically sort, file, mark, or manage incoming (or outgoing) communications. You instruct Outlook on what to look for and how to respond when it receives a message that satisfies the criteria you've established.

➢ **Right click on specific email – click Create Rule – create rule based on criteria you want set by** (by sender, recipient, or subject) **– decide what happens with email** (such as automatically moved to specific folder)

PROS	CONS
• Create rules to automatically redirect emails specifically to designated folder (based on sender, recipient, subject, etc.) • Search has the ability to search for messages in all folders	• If rule is too generic, messages could be classified incorrectly and harder to find • May not see email due to rule that moves email to a sub folder automatically, you may forget to see it/look for it

❖ **View messages as conversations – probably all folders** – groups messages together by subject line, allowing you to see (or collapse) the entire conversation back and forth, including sent items.

➢ **View tab – check Show as Conversations box**

PROS	CONS
• Easy to see how many messages are clustered together (indicated by triangle on left side of message) • Easy to see how many messages in cluster are still unread (bold number in parenthesis) • Helps to visually see that	• Must search in each cluster when looking for specific information further down in the message • Grouping by subject line removes the ability to easily find messages from a specific day or time period

you're responding to the most recent message	• Harder to see attachments in collapsed view

❖ **Use conversation Clean Up** – removes redundant messages (from messages such as Reply All, which duplicates the original message) and automatically moves the duplicative messages to the Deleted Items folder.

➢ **Folder tab – choose Clean Up Folder drop down menu – click Clean Up Folder and Subfolders – click Clean Up Folder**

PROS	CONS
• Purges duplicate information in emails (such as when reply emails contain the same exact information as the original email)	• Only purges messages that haven't been altered (such as messages that were replied to but erased filler content – like extra signature lines)

❖ **Edit the Subject line of an email** - to make searching more efficient, you can edit the Subject line making it more succinct with the topic (project name, initiative, specific task, etc.)

➢ **Double click on message to edit subject line (message needs to be popped out) – edit as needed – save message**

PROS	CONS
• Efficiently identify emails by their subject line, succinct to the topic • Enormously helpful (for instance if you have periodic signoff emails and need to identify by the subject, or project name)	• Altering original subject line

❖ **Mark email To Do** – What is the difference between tasks and To-Do list in Outlook? Tasks are a list of items you intend to complete. Any Outlook item marked for follow-up, typically marked email, as well as all of the tasks in the Task folders are considered To-Dos.

➤ **Mark the Flag option or right click email, hover over Categorize and choose color coded checkbox that indicates which category you would like this message in.**

➤ You can rename color categories to your preference in the File tab, click the Categorize drop down box, and click All Categories. You have the option to delete, rename, or create a new category and select color that corresponds with each category.

PROS	CONS
• Sort emails by color coded	• Not a good tool for

categories • Sort emails by flagged status • See list of flagged emails in To-Do tab (next to calendar) where you can assign due dates • Can create a separate task list not linked to emails (still not very robust though)	recurring tasks • Not robust enough to create multiple tasks for the same email

❖ **Flag messages – Located in For Follow Up Items folder -** you can monitor responses to emails you send by flagging them. Another option is to make sure you respond to communications you receive. A reminder alert is an option in both scenarios.

➢ **Click flag icon next to message – search Follow Up Items folder (under Search Folders section on left pane)**

PROS	CONS
• Flag messages in a group to refer to later	• May be difficult to sort by flagged messages once they've been archived

❖ **Create an Accomplishments Folder** – keep an organized list of accomplishments of note you'd like to refer back to (such as summaries of pain points, project milestones, or presentations you've created), you can have these emails in multiple folders but this allows you to quickly reference items you're particularly proud of.

➢ **Right click Inbox – create New Folder – name Accomplishments (or something applicable) – copy email – edit the subject line if necessary - manually drop items in folder (like summaries of pain points, project milestones, or presentations you've created);**

PROS	CONS
• Excellent way to recall measures of accomplishment, especially if they were sent via email • Quick reference folder for quarterly review meetings	• Manual process of dragging & dropping

❖ **Create a new Follow Up Folder to track emails you're expecting responses for** – there are many methods to following up on emails, I like this method because my items are not time bound by any specific time, but I still need to recall when I initially asked for a response.

➢ **Right click Inbox – create New Folder – name Follow Up (or something applicable) – manually drop items in folder to come back to (like sent messages with action items awaiting a response)**

PROS	CONS
• Great for quickly recalling items you're waiting on a response for	• Manual process to dragging & dropping • Manual process for moving back to Sent folder once you no longer need to be reminded

❖ **Color code meetings in Outlook Calendar -** you can color code meetings in Outlook based on different criteria, such as to highlight critical meetings or differentiate between mandatory and optional meetings, especially if they overlap.

➢ **Calendar - View tab – View Settings – click Conditional Formatting– click Add, Insert label (such as Mandatory Meetings) – select Color (Red) – click Condition – Type Town Hall (or another specific subject name) – click OK – click OK – Click OK**

➢ **Moving forward, once the Conditional Tag label has been created, you can Categorize a**

color code to the initial calendar meeting email and it will update the color in your calendar (bonus if it's a recurring meeting).

PROS	CONS
• Specific calendar meetings stand out (such as mandatory vs. optional) so you can choose which meeting to attend	• Need to manually set up conditional formatting • Adding too many colors may lose significance for specific meetings

~ Productivity tips – OneNote ~

❖ **Create checklists for projects -** Before starting a project, use a good preparatory check list to ensure that you don't neglect to complete any important activities.

➤ **In OneNote select Insert tab - choose table drop down - pick number of rows and columns (you can add/delete some later) - insert checklist items in each cell - highlight cells to insert To Do checkbox - Home tab - click To Do in Tags section (a new Layout tab will be visible allowing you to insert and delete rows along with other formatting tools to edit once the table has been created)**

➤ **Did you create a Contact List? If so, this would be an excellent place to put it so you can refer to it quickly.** *Pin OneNote to your Toolbar along with Outlook, Word, Excel, Edge, and other applications you reference frequently.*

PROS	CONS
• Create checklists to remind you what's been finished vs. items left to do • Have notes on multiple tasks/projects on individually named tabs	• Works best for recurring tasks but can be done for smaller lists as well (think of a grocery list)

On to the 3rd step, determining new (or expanding on our existing) skills to be qualified for a promotion or new job we're interested in. We have to identify our existing skills, both hard skills and soft skills. What distinguishes hard talents from soft skills? Hard skills are the knowledge and skills specific to a work that employees require to successfully carry out their obligations. On the other hand, soft skills are the character traits that actually enable employees to thrive at work. While soft skills reveal which of these applicants are also strong in person, hard skills aid in identifying individuals who are strong on paper. This indicates that for any individual to succeed in their position, there needs to be a solid balance between hard and soft abilities. Hard skills are acquired through schooling and on-the-job training, whereas soft skills are acquired through a variety of diverse, lifelong professional and personal experiences. For instance, marketing professionals can develop their teamwork abilities by joining a sports team, or they can study marketing strategies and tools by taking a marketing course.

Hard skills, sometimes referred to as technical skills, are position- and seniority-specific and job-specific. In other words, every job in every organization will need a different set of hard talents. For instance, a developer doesn't need to know how to reconcile financial statements, although an accountant must. Reconciliation is crucial for accountants of all experience levels, but creating corporate budgets is a skill that isn't typically expected of a beginning accountant.

Soft skills are broad traits that are connected to personality traits. Depending on the position or level of competence, you'd like to see certain soft skills in all employees, while other soft skills are more relevant in some roles and less so in others. For instance, if your business values collaboration, you should look for candidates that are excellent team players and have excellent communication skills. On the other hand, networking and relationship-building abilities could be necessary for jobs in sales and marketing but pointless for jobs in engineering. Similarly, leadership skills are appropriate for anyone managing a team, regardless of department.

View some examples of hard and soft skills in the chart then list a few of your own.

Hard skills	Yours?	**Soft skills**	Yours?
Adobe software suite	Data Analysis	Adaptability	Efficiency
Bilingual or multilingua.		Creativity	
Data mining		Critical thinking	
Database management		Dependability	
Marketing campaign management		Effective communication	
Mobile development		Empathy	
Programming languages (Python)		Open-mindedness	
SEO/SEM marketing		Organization	

Statistical analysis		Problem-solving	
Storage systems and management		Teamwork	
User interface design		Willingness to learn	

To recap,

- Concentrate on completing our existing duties and projects thoroughly, accurately, and on time. **Make a list of your current duties, include projects you've completed.**

- Look for ways to make those existing responsibilities more efficient so we can handle them with ease. **List those efficiencies and explain how they helped (learned something new, made tasks faster, improved functionality, etc.).**

- Determine new skills/tools we need to learn to be qualified for the promotion or new job) we're seeking. **Make a list of potential new skills you need to brush up on or learn to be qualified for your North Star position (think 5 years in the future what your skills would need to look like).** *Pay attention to not only the job description, but the specific hard and soft skills at the bottom of the job profile (make sure you can back up your skills with specific examples).* Skills you lack should be on your list of skills to learn/obtain. Keep in mind, some of your existing skills may be transferable but it's up to you to clearly draw that connection on your resume/cover letter using the terminology on the job description so you have a better chance at being selected for an interview.

Stop putting out fires means not letting things overwhelm you. Figure out ways to eliminate stress by approaching issues with whatever means necessary - picking your battles with kids/spouse/relationships, delegating/automating tasks, batching work together, destressing with something in your control, etc.

Additional Action Item: Deliberately learn something new every week, by the end of the year you will have learned 52 new things!

Chapter Six
Managing Up

The ability to manage one's superiors is vital, yet it's often disregarded in the workplace. It implies being able to anticipate, analyze, and respond strategically to your manager's requirements, even if they themselves are unsure of what those needs are.

Managing up is a concept in which an employee proactively takes responsibility for building and maintaining a positive relationship with their manager or supervisor. By effectively managing up, you can accelerate your career in several ways:

1. **Improving communication:** When you manage up, you prioritize communication with your manager. By regularly discussing your goals, challenges, and progress with your manager, you can ensure that you are aligned with your manager's expectations and can receive valuable feedback on your work. This can help you improve your skills and

productivity and can also help you avoid misunderstandings or mistakes that can impede your progress.

2. **Increasing visibility:** When you manage up, you become more visible to your manager and other senior leaders in your organization. This can help you gain recognition for your achievements, build a positive reputation, and position yourself for new opportunities or promotions. By showing initiative and demonstrating your value to the organization, you can gain the attention and support of key decision-makers, which can accelerate your career growth.

3. **Building trust:** When you manage up, you demonstrate that you are a reliable and trustworthy employee. This can help build trust and credibility with your manager, which can lead to more autonomy, responsibility, and leadership opportunities. By taking ownership of your work, proactively addressing challenges, and delivering results, you can earn your manager's confidence and respect, which can help you advance your career.

4. **Aligning with company goals:** When you manage up, you can gain a better

understanding of your organization's goals and priorities. This can help you align your work with the company's strategic direction and can position you as a valuable contributor to the organization's success. By showing that you are invested in the company's mission and vision, you can gain the support and mentorship of your manager and other senior leaders, which can help you accelerate your career.

Overall, managing up can help accelerate your career by improving communication, increasing visibility, building trust, and aligning with company goals. By actively cultivating a positive relationship with your manager and taking ownership of your work, you can position yourself for new opportunities and achieve greater success in your career.

First and foremost, take the initiative to come up with innovative ideas that solve your supervisor's core problems or challenges, rather than waiting to be told what needs to be done. Make sure to keep the lines of communication open by scheduling frequent meetings to discuss the status of ongoing initiatives and discuss potential new ones. Avoid confusion by communicating any potential stumbling blocks early on and by dividing down large tasks into smaller, more manageable chunks. Taking responsibility for your work is a great way to show how dedicated you are to the success of a project.

When you manage up well, you make your manager's (and your own) job easier. Knowing how to communicate effectively with your superiors, demonstrating empathy, meeting performance goals, and so on will all be considered. Managing upwards may become more important when working with a new manager or while switching teams. If you can immediately demonstrate these traits, it may help set your relationship on the right course.

Caring managers take an interest in their employees' personal lives and make an attempt to learn as much as they can about them. Managers-up are the ones who invest in getting to know their superiors. Demonstrate your concern for your manager's happiness and success by praising their efforts.

The Do's of managing up:

- Your manager may not need you to coach in the classic sense, but you can still provide constructive criticism like a coach.

- When asked what your manager can do to help you develop professionally, always respond truthfully. Think about this in advance so you can produce specific suggestions.

- One of the most productive ways to manage up is to learn your manager's preferred methods of communication. If you have a question that can't wait until your next scheduled one-on-one encounter, the best method to reach them is... If you focus on your manager's needs and actively listen to what they have to say, you will improve your ability to communicate with them.

- If you aspire to get into management ranks, you should learn about your boss's long-term goals. If your manager wants to move up the ranks and become the department's vice president someday, what can you do to make that happen? While your manager is keeping an eye on your own professional development, you should also look for methods to help and acknowledge the successes of your coworkers.

- Can you retain your cool, get work done, and adjust well to changing circumstances, even when you're feeling extremely pressured? Can you help your manager out while they're dealing with a lot of change and stress? You can't ask for a better way to manage up than this.

- If you see that your manager is getting overwhelmed, offer to take on more responsibility or assist with planning a team meeting. Also, you might express your willingness to take on more responsibility.

- Fair treatment of employees occurs when managers assign tasks while taking into account each worker's skills and professional goals. If you want to encourage fair treatment from your superiors, one thing you can do as a direct report is to provide them positive feedback when they do so.

- One of the most important things you can do to foster an atmosphere that encourages creativity is to avoid micromanagement. This is especially important when managing upwards, since no one wants to come across as micromanaging their boss.

- Gain insight from both your failures and triumphs, and let your superiors know how important it is for you to be trusted with considerable latitude in your work. Doing so will foster original thought.

- A manager who is doing a good job will be highly recommended by the employees under their supervision. Making your manager feel appreciated and having a stake in the company's success are two keys to good management of upwardly reports.

- Recognizing the importance of performance criteria and making sure they are met is one method to manage up when working for an outcomes-focused supervisor.

- Helping your coworkers achieve and maintain high performance standards is in everyone's best interest, including your boss's. Be a leader to your peers.

- If you are more technically savvy than your manager, you should help them improve in that area. You may have worked with a manager before, despite the fact that they may be woefully behind the technological curve, because such managers are not always easy to come by. Contribute some time teaching them how to use the latest gadgets. They likely possess other traits that make them qualified to lead.

- Do you get help from upper management in articulating the company's long-term goals and strategies in terms of daily tasks? Make them realize how much they mean to you by sharing your thoughts. When your management is sure that you understand how your role contributes to the organization as a whole, they will be free to concentrate on results.

The Do Not's of managing up:
- Complain
- Gripe
- Gossip
- Be judgmental
- Share too much personal information that could be construed as counterproductive

Unless you are a rocket scientist, there is generally more than one way to accomplish a given task. If you're ever feeling annoyed by the way your boss wants things done (or anyone else for that matter), try to think like a boss and remind yourself that there's usually more than one way to get the job done. Do you take the time to consider all perspectives in every situation? Managing up means you should be.

Managing up effectively will elevate your status, showcasing your willingness and ability to manage well, which could also put you on a short list for promotions when they become available.

Chapter Seven
Accomplishments Formula

Now that you've done some of the prep work of figuring out what your strengths and weaknesses are, it's time to get crystal clear on your accomplishments. Make a list of your organizations' goals – you'll need to tie your accomplishments to the bigger goal if possible. Also make a list of your departments' goals for the same reason, that's how you should back into your individual goals. The most effective goals will be SMART goals because they are Specific, Measurable, Attainable, Relevant, and Time-Bound which will help hold yourself accountable.

- **Specific** - It is essential to have a clear vision of what you want to accomplish. It's difficult to know exactly where — or on what — to spend one's efforts when there is a lack of clarity, or when there are multiple variables crammed into the pursuit of a single goal.

- **Measurable** - Including a definite indicator of progress in the pursuit of your objective makes it much simpler to determine whether or not the objective has been attained.

- **Attainable** - Establishing goals that can actually be achieved is crucial. It's good to set ambitious targets, but it can be discouraging to work toward something you have little chance of accomplishing.

- **Relevant** - Work must be focused where it will have the greatest impact on the company's bottom line. Don't squander resources on targets that aren't important to your organization's mission.

- **Time-Bound** - You should specify a specific deadline for when something needs to be done. It is crucial for gauging progress and inspiring continued effort.

Do you remember Mad Libs books where you had to insert random nouns, verbs, and adjectives that made for funny short stories? Let's look at an example.

Mad Lib Story
- · NOUN –
- · NOUN –
- · VERB –

- NOUN –
- ADJECTIVE –
- ADJECTIVE –
- ADJECTIVE –
- ADJECTIVE –
- PLURAL NOUN –
- NUMBER –

Now plug them in.

Dear Humans – it's me, (NOUN). Remember me? Your beloved (NOUN) who you left for two weeks to explore Italy? How could you do this to me?! You know I love adventures, especially ones that involve (VERB)! I thought we agreed after your last vacation trip to (NOUN), that you wouldn't vacation without me. I'll admit that I'm having a(n) (ADJECTIVE) time with grandma and grandpa at their house, but they don't have very good taste. They keep giving me (ADJECTIVE) food! Did you forget to tell me that I love (ADJECTIVE) bacon and juicy (ADJECTIVE)? I bring them (PLURAL NOUN) to throw so we can play fetch, but they only throw them about (NUMBER) times before they get tired.

Partial and simplified example from Ad Libs for Adults: *Laugh Your Blank Off!* (JBC Story Press, 2022).

While Mad Libs uses random verbs, adjectives, and nouns to create a funny story, we can create a similar formula for our needs. What we need is a formula that includes action verbs and SMART metrics to articulate our accomplishments. Refer to Appendix C for examples of action words, categorized by responsibilities.

<u>Formula</u>
(Action Verb) ___ (Metric) resulting in (Result) by (How)....

Another way is to start with the end result, and back into the steps it took to achieve it.

❖ **End goal:**
❖ **What steps went into achieving it:**
  o **1.**
  o **2.**
  o **3.**

Let's start with a basic goal and expand it with the criteria above, fill in the details with accurate metrics, be sure you can back up your claims with detailed facts, and more importantly, HOW you did it. We'll work thru a couple of examples:

Examples:

End goal: Helped create a new mentoring document that resulted in streamlining the process.

What steps went into achieving it:

- ➤ Copious note taking
- ➤ Developed specific contact list
- ➤ Documented step by step templates
- ➤ Decreased learning curve for new hires
- ➤ Freed resources allowing additional time to take on more responsibilities

SMART Goal: Developed a new mentoring document resulting in a more streamlined onboarding process and decreasing learning curve by 30%.

End Goal: Project Milestone – identified areas of optimization to support the milestone vision, reduce AHT, and enhance the agent experience.

Areas that need to expand on even further:

- ➤ Areas of optimization - # and what those specific areas were
- ➤ What was the higher AHT – what was the end AHT
- ➤ How did you enhance the agent experience?
- ➤ How you Influenced decision makers….

SMART Goal: Identified and maintained areas of operation eliminating bottleneck processes by 25%

resulting in project efficiencies enhancing the agent experience.

The XYZ method is a similar framework for writing accomplishment statements in a resume or CV. The name "XYZ" stands for "X achieved Y by doing Z."

Here's an example of how the XYZ method could be used to write an accomplishment:

X - Increased social media engagement by 25%
Y - Generated $50,000 in additional sales
Z - Created a new social media marketing campaign for a product launch.

Combining our XYZ gives us a thorough accomplishment that says: **Increased social media engagement by 25%, generating $50,000 in additional sales, by creating a new social media marketing campaign for a product launch.**

Let's break it down, here's how it works:

X - Start by describing the action you took to achieve a specific goal or task. This should be a concise and clear statement that explains what you did. For example:
    a. Increased sales revenue by 25%
    b. Reduced project timelines by 20%

    c. Won a regional award for outstanding customer service

Y - Next, describe the results or outcomes of your action. This should be specific and quantifiable, whenever possible. Use numbers or percentages to show the impact of your work. For example:
    a. Resulting in an additional $500,000 in annual revenue
    b. Resulting in increased productivity and cost savings
    c. Improving the company's reputation and customer satisfaction ratings

Z - Finally, describe the benefit of the results or outcomes to the organization or team. This should explain why your accomplishment matters and how it contributed to the success of the project or organization. For example:
    a. Developed and executed a new sales strategy targeting untapped markets
    b. Conducted a needs analysis and selected and implemented a new project management software
    c. Provided exceptional customer service by going above and beyond to solve complex problems

Then put them together:

A. Increased sales revenue by 25%, resulting in an additional $500,000 in annual revenue, by developing and executing a new sales strategy targeting untapped markets.

B. Reduced project timelines by 20%, resulting in increased productivity and cost savings, by conducting a needs analysis and implementing a new project management software.

C. Won a regional award for outstanding customer service, improving the company's reputation and customer satisfaction ratings, by providing exceptional customer service through going above and beyond to solve complex problems.

Using the XYZ method can help you showcase your achievements in a way that is clear, concise, and impactful. By focusing on the specific actions you took, the quantifiable results you achieved, and the impact it had on the organization, you can demonstrate your value and expertise to potential employers.

Below are some action-oriented examples to help you get started on articulating your accomplishments, make sure to expand on them to include all aspects of the SMART goal, especially metrics.

Customer Focused goals:
- Boosted customer outreach
- Decreased the percentage of returned products
- Expanded customer conversion rates
- Grew the number of new customers
- Improved customer satisfaction
- Increased customer retention
- Increased the number of returning customers
- Offered great customer value
- Penetrated new customer segments
- Reduced customer churn

Data goals:
- Automated processes
- Launched data driven products
- Plotted a success roadmap
- Restructured team

Finance goals:
- Attained and maintained profitability
- Became a financially sustainable company
- Diversified revenue streams
- Grew shareholder value
- Increased profit margin
- Increased revenue

- Influenced the percentage of local vs. international sales
- Reduced department-specific budgets
- Reduced production costs
- Set revenue targets for new products

Human Resource goals:
- Added X new team members
- Attracted top talent
- Built a healthy organizational culture
- Built better facilities management
- Built high-performing teams
- Designed employee-focused training programs
- Implemented a performance review cycle
- Improved cross-functional productivity
- Improved workplace safety
- Increased employee retention
- Invested in personal and professional development
- Reduced employee turnover
- Standardized processes
- Standardized titles and/or levels

Strategic Growth goals:
- Acquired a new company
- Broke into new markets
- Developed new products, features, or services
- Expanded brand on social media
- Improved company velocity

- Increased market share
- Increased operational reliability and/or compliance
- Opened new locations
- Surged website traffic

Of course, this is not a comprehensive list but notice the action verb in each example, feel free to use synonyms to avoid using the same words too many times on your resume.

Accomplishments aren't only good for resumes, they're imperative for periodic check-in's or reviews with your boss, when asking for a raise, or asking for a promotion. Use accomplishments to craft your personal pitch. When someone asks what you do, you don't want to ramble off a few job descriptions, instead highlight a recent project or two with impressive metrics

Chapter Eight
Building the 3-Dimensional Resume

You've done the hard part of articulating your accomplishments, now let's put all the pieces together to give our resume depth. By now you should have the following documents created: (1) A master list of categorized bullet point accomplishments **(Accomplishments List)**; (2) A master list of detailed accomplishments with bullet points listing how you accomplished them **(Detailed Accomplishments)**. If you don't have these lists ready, follow the steps below. These documents will be instrumental in deciding which accomplishments best represent the applicable skills you want to highlight on your resume, as well as keep a running list of all your previous accomplishments to choose from.

❖ Start with listing (in bullet point form) your **Accomplishments List**
  ○ Combine them in STAR format, if you can, to give the accomplishments teeth
❖ Categorize those accomplishments into overarching categories (such as leadership,

organization, management, project management, and so forth)

❖ Expand (in bullet point form) HOW you accomplished those feats and/or how they contributed to the bigger picture to create your **Detailed Accomplishments document**

Let's break this down even further so it's crystal clear.

Creating a professional accomplishments list can be a powerful tool to showcase your achievements and demonstrate your value to potential employers. Here are some steps to follow to create a professional accomplishments list:

1. **Brainstorm:** Begin by making a list of all the accomplishments you have achieved in your professional career so far. This list can include things like awards, promotions, successful projects, and other notable achievements.

2. **Identify measurable results:** When creating your accomplishments list, focus on accomplishments that have tangible and measurable results. This will help demonstrate the impact you have had in your role and provide concrete evidence of your skills and abilities.

3. **Use action-oriented language:** When describing your accomplishments, use strong action-oriented language that highlights your role in achieving the results. For example, instead of saying "contributed to a successful project," say "led a team that delivered a project ahead of schedule and under budget."

4. **Quantify your accomplishments:** Whenever possible, include specific numbers and metrics to quantify your accomplishments. This will help demonstrate the impact of your work and make your accomplishments more impressive.

Remember, a professional accomplishments list should be concise and focused on your most impressive achievements.

Next, categorize each bullet point in your list into over-arching categories so you can establish credibility with specific experience. For example, you may want to highlight experience pertaining to Leadership and then you would showcase 3 or so examples (with metrics) specifically relating to that skill.

1. **Categorize your accomplishments:** Organize your accomplishments into categories that make sense for your industry and role. This could include categories like leadership,

innovation, revenue growth, or customer satisfaction.

Detailed Skills

Data Analysis:
- Advanced knowledge of Microsoft Excel 2010, 2013, & 2016 formulas and functions, such as Pivot Table, What-If Analysis, VLOOKUP function, etc., and drill-down Dashboards
- Experience with CRM, ERP, and POS Software, such as Eclipse, SAP, Microsoft Dynamics GP & SL, SBA, and Salesforce, as well as task management tools
- Experience with Power B and Tableau software

Managerial Consulting:
- Analytical breakdown of business processes to develop solutions, recommend process improvements to increase productivity, as well as train staff on program use and optimization
- Conducted organizational study for an organization; presented results and recommendations in a strategic analysis report with drill-down dashboards for stakeholders
- Collected and analyzed data using calculations, graphical projection models, and other methods as necessary to understand current operations and determine areas for improvement

Project Management:
- Strategically developed working relationships at all levels to build consensus
- Coordinated events and logistics with advanced preparation as well as adeptly set and tracked project costs and productivity benchmarks
- Collected and analyzed data using calculations, graphical projection models, and other methods as necessary to understand current operations and determine areas for improvement

---

Lastly, I recommend creating a copy of the Accomplishments List so you can expand on HOW you accomplished the specific feat and/or what the impact was. Basically, you're elaborating on accomplishments for interview purposes so you have a list of examples to choose from, picking one's that are relevant to the position you're seeking. Don't forget to keep this list up to date by adding accomplishments periodically.

Analytics Experience

Board & Employee Survey

- Analyzed a non-numerical organizational survey, consisting of employees and board members; presented results and recommendations in a strategic analysis report for stakeholders; results of the analysis are being used to inform 5 year strategic plan |
    - Took raw survey that asked for two or more answers and manually separated them into singular answers for comparison
    - Categorized each answer into overarching themes
    - Assigned each singular answer a positive or negative disposition
    - Proceeded to analyze based on context and frequency of recurring themes

Improved Payroll Process

- Improved payroll and HR functionality, including maintaining career/job trajectory tracking, benchmarking professional staff development, assessing performance appraisals year over year, and created a system to efficiently track annual data for the end of year employee contribution reports.
    - Reduced payroll process from several days to mere minutes utilizing complex formulas and macros.

You may not need all this information but having a detailed master list of your categorized accomplishments will help you tailor your resume as well as prepare you for interviews. We've been piecing this out but now let's put it all together.

Think of these documents as layers and each layer explains your point in more detail, helping you articulate your value in succinct and deliberate ways, *at the right time*. Remember, your resume merely touches on a particular accomplishment (categorized so we can batch similar accomplishments together), further driving home our direct experiences. If done correctly, our resume checks all the boxes of being qualified, getting past the gatekeepers, and into the hands of a hiring manager who decides to interview us for the role. The detailed list of our accomplishments helps us articulate the impact we had with metrics that enhance credibility. I don't know about you, but sometimes I have a difficult time coming up with details on an older accomplishment on the spot so I have to jot them down. I work on too many projects to remember pertinent details from projects in the past.

The categorized Accomplishments List informs the pertinent accomplishments you want to highlight on your resume. The Detailed Accomplishments document is used to prepare for the interview process.

The resume should draw a clear conclusion that you'd be a good fit for the position you're seeking based on your experience, if it doesn't tell that story, you may need to continue refining your resume.

I was an accountant for many years, and a tax preparer for even longer, that meant that my resume screamed Accounting, even though I didn't want to be an accountant anymore. I was looking for a way to reword my resume so it would show more data analysis experience, which took many years of refining my resume and strategic word art. It was also necessary to work on cross departmental projects and look for opportunities to take on more of what I wanted to do simply for the sake of my resume. What

I did was volunteer for any opportunity that would help bolster my resume and/or give me new experiences, then I purposefully added them to my portfolio. Slowly, but surely, I was able to replace some of my accounting accomplishments with data analysis experience accomplishments as well as use multiple job titles to distinguish my experience.

Piece together the sections of your new resume and hopefully it's telling the story you're trying to convey.

Mickey Mouse, MBA

Orlando, Florida ▪ 555-666-7777
MickeyMouseMBA@hotmail.com ▪ www.linkedin.com/in/mickey-mouse-mba

---

SENIOR ANALYST | STRATEGY ANALYST | REPORTING CONSULTANT | DIRECTOR OF CORPORATE STRATEGY

Results-driven, growth-oriented professional with 10+ years' experience in business management and non-profit civic organizations. Expert at planning and setting long-term strategic plans, as well as optimizing organizational efficiency, reducing cost, and surpassing business objectives. Recently analyzed an organizational survey for the future direction of the organization; presented results and recommendations in a strategic analysis report for stakeholders; results of the analysis were used to inform 5-year strategic plan.

Highlights of Expertise

• Strategic Forecasting and Planning	• Experience with Power BI & Tableau	• Microsoft Access
• Project Management skills	• Strategy and Program Evaluation	• Benchmark Productivity
• Advanced Microsoft Excel skills	• Advanced Excel & Data Analytics	• Dashboard Building

---

Education

Master of Business Administration	12/2017	*University of Central Florida, Orlando, FL*
Bachelor of Public Administration	5/2015	*University of Central Florida, Orlando, FL*
Associate of Accounting & Business Administration	6/2012	*University of Central Florida, Orlando, FL*

Does it highlight the skills you need for your future position? Does it highlight direct experience related to your future position? Does your resume and the desired job description meet or exceed the 80% match rate at JobScan.com? Refer to Appendix D for sample resumes that utilize this format. See how it meets the eye test, what sections draw your attention first? Hiring managers are likely going to notice the same sections first too.

Jobscan.com is a web-based software that scans your resume and job description to give you a match rate based on hard and soft keywords. I highly recommend referring to this resource before submitting a job application as it will give you a good idea of how qualified of a match you are for the position.

Chapter Nine
Professional Tips

Pain Point Cover Letters are a strategic way to articulate that you understand an issue they are likely facing as well as position yourself as the solution to that problem. This is done by communicating how you can specifically solve their problem based on your past experience/results. You want the potential employer or hiring manager to read this and say, "Yes, this person is exactly who we need!" Cover letters are a good place to elaborate on a specific accomplishment as if you were responding to a pain point issue you identified (or presumed) for the company – stay in your lane though, the perceived company probably needs to be something in your wheelhouse (such as an accounting issue if you're seeking an accounting role or marketing issue if you're seeking a marketing role).

To begin, think about the issue that would be addressed by your addition to the team. Obtain the job description and study its details. Go over each responsibility and think about why the organization might want or need someone to take care of that role. Are they expanding at an alarming rate? Is this a newly created position or did someone quit or get fired? The job description should, but does not always, highlight the most important functions of the role so you should tailor your cover letter to convey your experience solving one or more of those issues. Pain Point Cover Letters are another way to tailor your documents for a specific role.

Interviewing Tips – Confidence is key to interviewing because when you take the perspective of utilizing your skills (think of yourself like a consultant), you are providing a skill set they need. Employers are literally telling you a need they have by posting the job in the first place, when you think of yourself as the solution for their pain point (what skills have they articulated a need for in the job description?), you can present yourself as the solution by highlighting your skills/experience to fill that role.

This mindset of considering yourself a consultant with relevant skills involves taking a step back, asking thoughtful questions, and projecting confidence in one's abilities. It demonstrates your business acumen and your willingness to take the initiative to implement change. It's noticeable and memorable when it matters most: at the time of narrowing down candidates.

If you were a consultant, you would probe to better understand the problems that this company is facing, such as asking about workflow, competition, sales hurdles, etc. Concurrently, you are promoting yourself and your abilities to potential employers. Therefore, as they talk about company problems, you reveal your own experience and credentials by asking questions or by explaining how you have handled similar situations.

An ordinary interviewee can be transformed into a supreme one by adopting a consulting mindset. If you take on a consultative stance, you'll be better able to ask pointed questions and hone in on the root causes of their problems, which will lead you to the kinds of solutions they'll like, making you more memorable when they make the final hiring decision.

Likeability – positivity and gratitude go a long way. Skills matter, but studies show that likeability can make up for a lack of skills, which can often be taught, but the right attitude shows whether or not you're trainable.

We'd all like to think that, when a position opens up, it's filled by the most qualified and deserving candidate. But put yourself in the hiring manager's shoes: would you rather hire someone you like but who requires some time to adjust to the job, or someone you don't care for but who has all the qualifications? Many people going into interviews have the misconception that they don't need to market themselves because they already have the necessary skills. They feel that their work speaks for itself and that should be sufficient enough. Perhaps, but that won't cut it with interviewers.

Likeability traits include, but are not limited to, dressing the part, acting genuinely interested in other people, staying actively engaged in the interview, asking pertinent questions, being mindful of your body language, and remaining pleasantly positive. This is especially important during an interview because first impressions can make or break a snap opinion about your ability to fit in with the company.

You'll want to come out as personable and approachable during the interview. Quickly, or else. Likeability, or how well you might mesh with the existing team, is a criteria that is at least as important as any other when it comes to the hiring decision. Yes, your skills, background, and history of success are crucial. It's true that there are always other qualified applicants out there. Individuality can come from intangible qualities like charm and charisma. Aptitudes are what get you the interviews but being memorable, and therefore likable, can get you hired.

Communication – Practice short, clear, and concise communication. GET TO THE POINT. Your boss will appreciate someone who gives a clear summary of what they need or what they're working on without beating around the bush or giving them useless information. Bosses, and colleagues alike, are busy so practice getting to the point. If you find you have a tendency to ramble, practice writing down what needs to be said first and then say only that. If you're in a meeting and always have comments or need to interject your own story, practice refraining from saying anything at all. Let others speak, saying less actually makes what you have to say more impactful if you're only speaking when you have something to contribute. Practicing your communication skills can lead to better opportunities as well.

Chapter Ten
Conclusion

Using the techniques in this book will significantly improve your resume as well as elevate your professional reputation, setting you apart from the competition and boosting your chances of receiving more interviews or being fast tracked for promotions. Make sure you're clear on your goals as that will make it easier to spot opportunities perfect for you. Identify your North Star goal then actively work on getting there, looking for opportunities, or better yet, creating them! Make sure you create a good system for tracking your accomplishments, eventually you'll want to use them for bragging about metrics or utilizing them in a portfolio, both of which will bolster your career. Keep in mind your resume is telling a story, it should draw a clear conclusion about how your past experience makes you qualified for the position you're seeking, if it doesn't make that clear, you may need to go back to the drawing board and reword your accomplishments (or leave off unrelated ones).

Go through the steps in Appendix A & B to gain clarity in your career plan and then take deliberate actions to achieve it. Of course, there are more advanced techniques to finding a job, such as targeting specific companies that you're well suited for, as well as other techniques, but this book gives you the fundamental foundation to stand out amongst your competition.

In order to be selected for an interview, you'll need to get past the gatekeepers (ATS bots), the tips in this book will greatly improve your chances. Do you want to gauge how good of a candidate you really are? Plug your resume and job description into JobScan.com; if you're about to get more than an 80% match rate, and you're one of the first few candidates to apply, you stand an exceedingly good chance of being selected for an interview (assuming the job isn't already earmarked for someone specific).

If you found any part of this book helpful, please consider posting a review wherever you purchased this book as well as share it with a friend. The greatest gift you can give is the gift of knowledge. I aim to enrich the lives with others through the information contained as knowledge is power.

~ BONUS ~

Resume Template

Get access to the formatted resume examples in this book. With these templates, you can edit and fill in with your own information. These are the same templates I have used to help others get high paying jobs. They are specially formatted to be aesthetically pleasing to the eye, highlight relevant accomplishments, and draw attention to the most pertinent information hiring managers look for. With carefully considered left, center, and right margins, these layouts make the most of the space available to showcase your value.

https://ElevateYourResume.com

Download the editable resume that fits your needs and begin plugging in your information. Change the font color from red to black once you've completed each section to indicate all the information contained has been updated to your own information. **Transform your mediocre resume into an impressive marketing document that impressively articulates your value!**

Appendix A

Vision Board

~ Goal Digger ~

Personal

Financial

Professional

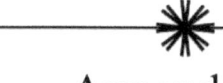

Appendix B
<u>SWOT Analysis</u>

Strengths	Weaknesses
1	1
2	2
3	3
4	4
5	5
How do you use them? Who do these skills benefit and how? How can you expand these strengths to be even more impactful?	Why are these holding you back? How can you practice turning these into strengths? What is the result of these weaknesses holding you back?

Tools You Utilize	New Tools You Could Try
1	1
2	2
3	3
4	4
5	5
What do you like about these tools? What do you dislike about these tools? What can you do to make these tools more efficient?	How would you utilize them? What would they improve? What is holding you back from trying these?

Appendix C
Action Words to Get You Started

Action verbs to describe saving time or money

* Conserved
* Consolidated
* Decreased
* Deducted
* Diagnosed
* Lessened
* Reconciled
* Reduced
* Yielded

Action verbs to describe changing or improving

* Centralized
* Clarified
* Converted
* Customized
* Influenced
* Integrated
* Merged
* Modified
* Overhauled
* Redesigned
* Refined
* Refocused
* Rehabilitated
* Remodeled
* Reorganized
* Replaced
* Restructured
* Revamped
* Revitalized
* Simplified
* Standardized
* Streamlined
* Strengthened
* Transformed
* Updated
* Upgraded

Action verbs to describe increasing revenue and sales

* Accelerated
* Achieved
* Advanced
* Amplified
* Boosted
* Capitalized
* Delivered
* Enhanced
* Expanded
* Expedited
* Furthered
* Gained
* Generated
* Improved
* Lifted
* Maximized
* Outpaced
* Stimulated
* Sustained

Action verbs to describe supporting customers

* Advised
* Advocated
* Arbitrated
* Coached
* Consulted
* Educated
* Fielded
* Informed
* Resolved

Action verbs to describe negotiating a deal

* Acquired
* Forged
* Navigated
* Negotiated
* Partnered
* Secured

Action verbs to describe leading a project

* Chaired
* Controlled
* Coordinated
* Executed
* Headed
* Operated
* Orchestrated
* Organized

* Oversaw
* Planned
* Produced
* Programmed

Action verbs to describe managing a project

* Administered
* Built
* Charted
* Created
* Designed
* Developed
* Devised
* Engineered
* Established
* Formalized
* Formed
* Formulated
* Founded
* Implemented
* Incorporated
* Initiated
* Instituted
* Introduced
* Launched
* Pioneered
* Spearheaded

Action verbs to describe managing a team

* Aligned
* Cultivated
* Directed
* Enabled
* Facilitated
* Fostered
* Guided
* Hired
* Inspired
* Mentored
* Mobilized
* Motivated
* Recruited
* Regulated
* Shaped
* Supervised
* Taught
* Trained
* Unified
* United

Action verbs to describe researching

* Analyzed
* Assembled

* Assessed
* Audited
* Calculated
* Discovered
* Evaluated
* Examined
* Explored
* Forecasted
* Identified
* Interpreted
* Investigated
* Mapped
* Measured
* Qualified
* Quantified
* Surveyed
* Tested
* Tracked

Action verbs synonymous with communicating

* Collaborated
* Highlighted
* Reported

Action verbs synonymous with achieving results

* Accomplished
* Generated
* Identified
* Improved
* Increased
* Strengthened

Action verbs articulating influencing others

* Authored
* Briefed
* Campaigned
* Co-authored
* Composed
* Conveyed
* Convinced
* Corresponded
* Counseled
* Critiqued
* Defined
* Documented
* Edited
* Illustrated
* Lobbied
* Persuaded
* Promoted
* Publicized

* Reviewed

Action verbs articulating accomplishments
* Attained
* Awarded
* Completed
* Demonstrated
* Earned
* Exceeded
* Outperformed
* Reached
* Showcased
* Succeeded
* Surpassed
* Targeted

Action verbs synonymous with regulating
* Authorized
* Blocked
* Delegated
* Dispatched
* Enforced
* Ensure
* Inspected
* Itemized
* Monitored
* Screened
* Scrutinized
* Verified

Action verbs synonymous with assessing
* Analyzed
* Assembled
* Assessed
* Audited
* Calculated
* Discovered
* Evaluated
* Examined
* Explored
* Forecasted
* Identified
* Interpreted
* Investigated
* Mapped
* Measured
* Qualified
* Quantified
* Surveyed
* Tested
* Tracked

Action verbs synonymous with leading

* Aligned
* Cultivated
* Directed
* Enabled
* Facilitated
* Fostered
* Guided
* Hired
* Inspired
* Mentored
* Mobilized
* Motivated
* Recruited
* Regulated
* Shaped
* Supervised
* Taught
* Trained
* Unified
* United

Action verbs articulating general achievements

* Accomplished
* Achieved
* Advanced
* Constructed
* Coached
* Contracted
* Delivered
* Directed
* Exceeded
* Executed
* Enhanced
* Enlarged
* Established
* Improved
* Initiated
* Increased
* Innovative
* Oversaw
* Succeeded
* Supervised
* Super headed

Action verbs articulating analytical skills

* Analyzed
* Assembled
* Assessed
* Coached
* Constructed
* Corrected

* Created
* Defined
* Designed
* Developed
* Devised
* Diagnosed
* Established

* Evaluated
* Examined
* Fostered
* Installed
* Produced
* Programmed
* Solved

Donald D. Duck

Orlando, FL 32789 ▪ 800-555-5555
DonaldDDuck@gmail.com ▪ linkedin.com/in/Donald-D-Duck

Professional Profile

Highly experienced professional ready to translate leadership talents into a high-level management role.

Transformation-minded professional with grounded business leadership experience and a strong drive to leverage vision and strategic talents, devising and delivering bottom-line solutions for companies in competitive industries. Highly motivated to share business knowledge and solve problems proactively with efficiency and integrity for productive results, having more than 13 years' experience in automotive production, 6 years' experience working with gas and steam turbines, and a total of 35 years' experience in the manufacturing industry.

Highlights of Expertise

- Assembly Line Operations
- Machinery Assembly
- Performance Optimization
- Contract Management Negotiation

- Schematic Diagrams and Blueprints
- Production Line Efficiency
- Precision Component Assembly
- Safety Standards

- Quality Controls
- Critical Precision
- Cooperative Team Building
- Inventory Management

Direct Experience

Project Management:
- Adept at Setting and tracking project costs and productivity benchmarks
- Strategically develop working relationships at all levels to build consensus
- Proven ability to work under time and budget constraints while still maintaining quality products

Quality Assurance:
- Developed Standard Operation Procedures (SOS) for quality and efficiency purposes
- Collected and compiled statistical quality data for analysis
- Developed, recommended, and monitored corrective and preventative actions producing cost savings measures

Team Leadership:
- National trainer for at least 12 different installation components and processes for hundreds of technicians over a six-year span still currently in use, resulting in ongoing instruction
- Top 10% of employees chosen to participate in focus group meetings concerning ergonomics and line production efficiencies
- Trained ~40 supervisors, line-leaders, and technicians on improved paint processes

Certifications & Licenses

✓ Installation of seal strips RD3, RD5, RD10, RD18, and RD20
✓ Installation of all stages of blading on rotors and locking systems
✓ Installation of Steam blading carriers and diaphragms
✓ GT blading, CVC1, CVC2, TVC, compressor blading, and heat shields

✓ Forklift operator
✓ Overhead crane and rigging
✓ 9000 ISO & 14,000 ISO
✓ LOTO Safety Implementation

Professional Experience

Power Electric   Orlando, Florida

Trained and built turbine engines for the gas and steam power industry, monitored quality control procedures, and interpreted blueprint schematics.

TURBINE BLADE MACHINIST   August 2010 to October 2016
Travelled nationally and internationally for extended amounts of time to receive specialized training and certifications, including Germany, Switzerland, and Canada while continuously receiving promotions from Blading Assistant to Blader to GT Assembler. Frequent team lead for field service projects.

- National trainer for at least 12 different installation components and processes for hundreds of technicians over a six-year span still currently in use, resulting in ongoing instruction.
- Collaborated consistently with organization managers to identify performance gaps and devise solutions.
- Validates quality processes by establishing product specifications and quality attributes, measuring production, documenting evidence, determining operational and performance qualification, and writing and updating quality assurance procedures.

Ford North America   Orlando, Florida

Assembled various engines, diagnostic testing for troubleshooting issues, and performed corrective measures to meet quality standards.

PRODUCTION TECHNICIAN   January 2002 to January 2010

Tested products and subassemblies for functionality and quality, troubleshot problems with equipment, devices and products, and monitored and adjusted production processes of equipment for quality and productivity.

- Met and exceeded quotas resulting in cost and time management.
- Tested and diagnosed engines for critical feedback for preventative defects.
- Top 10% of employees chosen to participate in focus group meetings concerning ergonomics and line production efficiency.

Ford Auto Assembly Plant   Orlando, Florida

Identified and repaired defects, determined effective paint procedures, and provided critical feedback concerning quality.

PAINT PLANT TECHNICIAN   May 1997 to December 2002

Inspected for paint defects, identified problems and implemented solutions, and trained for optimal paint procedures.

- Trained ~40 supervisors, line-leaders, and technicians on improved paint processes.
- Assured ongoing compliance with quality and industry regulatory requirements.
- Reviewed the implementation and efficiency of quality and inspection systems utilizing the VES system.

Siskin Steel and Supply Co., Inc.   Orlando, Florida

Maintaining documents for shipping and receiving orders, sustained inventory control, and involved in the coordination of contract logistics.

INVENTORY MANAGER   October 1987 to May 1997

Inspected and verified the quality of product shipments, assessed supply and demand, and analyzed data to anticipate future needs.

- Implemented racking system that resulted in efficiencies in product fulfillment and safety measures.
- Managed contract logistics, forecasted order quantities, and maintained inventory levels.
- Reviewed the implementation and efficiency of quality and inspection systems utilizing the TED system.

Key & Son Refractory   Orlando, Florida

Installation and removal of fire brick for furnaces, and kilns.

INSTALLATION TECHNICIAN   June 1982 to October 1987

Served existing accounts by analyzing work orders, planning daily travel schedule, investigating complaints, conducting tests, and resolving problems.

- National travel and installation of smokestacks and high temperature furnaces.
- Pre-installation inspections and general scope of work recommendations that resulted in preventative costs.
- Reviewed the implementation and efficiency of quality and inspection systems utilizing the MLK system.
- Tested and diagnosed engines for critical feedback for preventative defects.

Mickey Mouse, Jr., MBA

Orlando, FL 37421 • 800-555-5555
MickeyMMouse@hotmail.com • www.linkedin.com/in/mickey-m-mouse

---

BRAND STRATEGY ASSOCIATE | STRATEGY ANALYST | ANALYTICAL CONSULTANT | DIRECTOR OF OPERATIONS

Recently analyzed an organizational survey for the future direction of the organization; presented results and recommendations in a strategic analysis report for stakeholders; results of the analysis were used to inform 5-year strategic plan. Frequently collect and analyze data using calculations, graphical project models, and other methods as necessary to understand current operations and determine areas for improvement. Excellent communication skills, adept at influencing key stakeholders, and the innate ability to create positive outcomes while helping others.

Highlights of Expertise

• Business Process Improvement	• Data Analytical Skills	• Program Management
• Brand Strategy	• Strategy and Program Evaluation	• Market Research
• Business Insights	• Performance Optimization	• Project Management Skills
• Quantitative Research	• Excellent Presentation Skills	• PowerPoint Skills
• Build Knowledge Base	• Business Process Prioritization	• Management Consulting

Education

Master of Business Administration	12/2017	*Florida University, Orlando, FL*
Bachelor of Public Administration	5/2015	*Florida University, Orlando, FL*
Associate of Accounting & Business Administration	6/2012	*Florida Community College, Orlando, FL*

Direct Experience

Analytics:
- Created multi-functional business development plan to engage and retain current members as well as provide additional tangible value
- Led organization to improve productivity by 30% through providing technical and performance-focused program development and training
- Collaborated with talented senior leaders to develop policies as well as action plans, implement programs, program events, and manage large-scale improvement projects
- Seamlessly handled full scope of planning, activities coordination, and execution of marketing and training events for contractors to earn certifications through marketing events and presentations

Brand Management:
- Analyzed demographic & economic market data to identify trends and forecast effective strategies
- Conducted organizational study, including data collection, analysis, and feedback; presented results and recommendations in a strategic analysis report for future strategic planning purposes
- Improved payroll and HR functionality, including, but not limited to, maintaining career/job trajectory tracking, benchmarking professional staff development, assessing performance appraisals year over year, and created a system to efficiently track annual data for the end of year employee contribution reports.
- Automated processes to increase efficiency and create capacity to take on additional projects

Project Management:
- Coordinated events and logistics of business requirements with advanced preparation as well as adeptly set and tracked project costs and productivity benchmarks
- Collected and analyzed data using calculations, graphical projection models, and other methods as necessary to understand current operations and determine areas for improvement
- Developed and updated system procedures as needed to address changing operational requirements and documented changes; tested procedures to keep system information accurate and productive
- Developed a step-by-step checklist template for each installation type for effectiveness as well as provide training, speeding up the learning curve

Professional Experience

NorthStar Orlando, Florida
NorthStar is comprised of the data side of Insurance and serves as a leader for data-driven, innovative solutions, such as Pharmacy+, Benefits Management+, Care+, Intelligence+.

LEAD ANALYST July 2021 to Present

Coordinate with insurance account team and vendors/clients to implement the ingestion of 6+ external data types for utilization in 20 downstream systems that support disease management/wellness programs, member incentives, analytics, predictive modeling, reporting, and new product offerings.

- Developed a step-by-step checklist template for each installation type for effectiveness as well as training.
- Efficiently set up hyperlinked emails for recurring communication.
- Lead a group of professionals in Lean-In Circle focusing on personal and professional development skills.

Orlando Economics Orlando, Florida
Coordinate with senior managers and colleagues to ensure effective data and financial support analysis and reporting.

ACCOUNTANT | STRATEGIC PLANNING ANALYST December 2014 to July 2021

Provided analytical breakdown of business processes to develop solutions, recommended process improvements to increase productivity for Chamber of 2,000+ business members, and staff of ~40. Support membership programs and strategize effective revenue streams. Promote economic development.

- Tracked and managed budget of $6M revenue/expenses for 2,000+ business members, 3 companies, ~40 staff, 15 depts., 14 councils, & 7 major events annually.
- Managed budgets, balance sheets, accounts payable & receivable, and monitor profit and loss of events.
- Improved payroll and HR functionality, including, but not limited to, maintaining career/job trajectory tracking, benchmarking professional staff development, assessing performance appraisals year over year, and created a system to efficiently track annual data for the end of year employee contribution reports.
- Devised benchmarking metric tracking system for Strategic Plan with drill-down dashboard to gauge strategic direction and monitor continuous improvement in real time.

Jackson Hewitt Tax Service Orlando, Florida
Managed all daily processes to ensure efficient and effective tax preparation for tax service clients seasonally as well as managed employees' schedules and mentored less experienced tax preparers.

TAX MANAGER January 2006 to April 2015

Supervised team of up to ~30 in preparing taxes, communicating with clients (individual, partnerships, small business), and handling daily administration of tax preparation service. Trained and mentored staff on all facets of tax analysis and preparation.

- Expertly provided technical resolutions for complex financial tax issues for individuals and small businesses.
- Led organization to improve productivity by 30% through providing technical and performance-focused training.
- Seamlessly researched and managed complex issues including collation and release of proprietary client data.

Robert Half & Accounting Orlando, Florida
Provided accounting services to client companies in manufacturing and transportation business sectors.

ACCOUNTING MANAGER May 2013 to December 2014

Managed accounting data, journal entries, and reports related to client's daily business operations. Reviewed documents, receipts, and invoices. Created and disseminated financial analysis reports.

- Skillfully identified and reconciled $2M in uncollected accounts receivables.
- Improved profit by increasing collection procedures, direct result of reduced bad debt by 200% weekly.
- Contributed to improving billing processes for clients by correcting issues and errors in collections data.

Wholesale Orlando, Florida
Held concurrent responsibility for overseeing branch operations while promoting sales to clients and coordinating events.

ACCOUNT EXECUTIVE & INTERIM BRANCH MANAGER April 2006 to April 2008

Supervised, managed, and trained team of 12 for efficiency on POS software. Collaborated with senior leaders to develop policies as well as action plans, implement programs, program events, and manage large-scale improvement projects.

- Seamlessly handled full scope of planning, activities coordination, and execution of marketing of training events as well as warranty claims for improved employee and customer service.
- Managed pricing and contract negotiations, forecasted order quantities, and performed cost analyses.

About the Author

I've been writing resumes for almost 20 years, fine tuning my method and experimenting with what works and what doesn't work. Over the years I've evolved my template (as one should always be doing) and now have a template that has a fairly high success rate of getting past the gatekeepers and getting noticed by the recruiters enough to get an interview. While the applicants themselves had to ace the interview, my resumes have helped many people get the interview for very high paying jobs (some paying more than $100,000 annually).

As a first-generation MBA graduate, I've worked very hard to climb the ranks in my business pursuits. I've reached a point in my career where I have gained the knowledge and ability to turn around and help the next group of ambitious professionals behind me.